A Few More Minutes

A Few More Minutes

A Poetry Collection

Brenda Livingston Bradley

Copyright © 2019 by Brenda Livingston Bradley.

Library of Congress Control Number:		2019914832
ISBN:	Hardcover	978-1-7960-6131-4
	Softcover	978-1-7960-6130-7
	eBook	978-1-7960-6132-1

All rights reserved. No part of this book may be reproduced or transmitted in any form or by any means, electronic or mechanical, including photocopying, recording, or by any information storage and retrieval system, without permission in writing from the copyright owner.

Any people depicted in stock imagery provided by Getty Images are models, and such images are being used for illustrative purposes only. Certain stock imagery © Getty Images.

Print information available on the last page.

Rev. date: 10/01/2019

To order additional copies of this book, contact:
Xlibris
1-888-795-4274
www.Xlibris.com
Orders@Xlibris.com

This book is lovingly dedicated to

Hannah and Isaac, my prayed-for children,
who challenge and inspire me

Randall, my husband and best friend, who supports,
encourages, and loves me unconditionally

ACKNOWLEDGMENT

Without a community of friends, this book would not have happened. Therefore, I want to thank my many friends and colleagues who have encouraged me to compile my poetry for publication. I am grateful to my friends from CCTE (Conference of College Teachers of English) for the opportunities to read my poems and receive their encouragement and input. I thank Jim McKeown who has read and critiqued many of my poems through the years. A special appreciation goes to Jeffrey DeLoto who encouraged me to pursue publishing and introduced me to Xlibris. I am grateful to Linda Cook who helped me categorize the poems and to Terry York, Elaine White, and Linda Cook who were each instrumental in helping me imagine a title. Most of all, I thank my family who have been my constant cheerleaders through the years – providing encouragement, listening to and critiquing first drafts, and especially providing subject matter for my poetry.

Contents

PART I
SEASONS
NATURE

Abundance	1
Fermata	2
Approaching Storm	3
Change of Seasons	4
Stopping by Bluebonnets on a Sunday Morning	5
Papa's Scuppernongs	6
Meet Me in St. Louis at Park Avenue	7
Blackberry Picking	8

LOSS

Mourning on Nanny's Porch	11
Streetlights	12
Cleaning Your Closet	13
Zippy Doodle	14
Caught Between Two Griefs	15
As You Lay Dying	16
Song 88	17
The Power of a Smile	18
Slaughter of Innocents	19
A Thin Line	20
Unnoticed	21
Visitation	22
Empty Spaces	23
Summer Fruit	24
The Garden	25
I Want to Buy You Pretty Things	26
On Joy in the Morning	27

Not a Door 28
The Waiting Room 29
'Mid Tubes and Blankets 30

FAITH

Advent 33
Not Yet 34
Among the Ashes 35
Yahweh 36
For This Moment 37
Faint as a Frightened Bird 38
Dust 39
Before the Dawn 40
Baraka za Mungu 41
Sometimes We Wait 42
Blessing 43
Breath of God 44

MEMORY

Pool in Decatur 47
Corner of Lee and 35 48
Worry Stories 49
Life in the Shadows 50
Broken Silence 51
Valley and Shadows 52
Scriptwriter 53
Sharp Memories 54
Starbucks Run 55
The Longing 56

TIME

The Bon Fire 59
Running South 60

My Life Will Go On 61
They May Never Be Remembered 62
Cracking Innocence 63
She Sent You Away to Pick Strawberries 64
Clay Pot 65
In the Meantime 66
Biscuits and Hot Coffee 67
Horseflies and Butterflies 68
Numbered Sunrises 69
Noticing Time 70
Mending Fences 71
Master Betrayer 72
Magnolias and Blue Bottles 73
Hotwheels and Invitations 75
Homeworker 76
Early Years Revisited 77
Somebody's Little Boy 78
Copper Strand 79

RELATIONSHIPS

Anniversary 83
In the Garden 84
Everybody's Got a Little Hot Pink Toe Polish in 'Em! 85
Under the Hackberry 86
The Farmhouse 88
Afternoons and Coffeespoons 89
The 5th Afternoon 90
Woodway Park II 92
One Day 93
Upon the Occasion of Your High School Graduation:
June 1, 2012 94
Evening in Calvert 95
In the Heat of the Day 96
On the San Antonio Riverwalk 97

Abandonment 98
Ten Steps Ahead 99
Rights 100
From the Balcony 101
Fierce Love 102

MISCELLANEOUS

Being Mindful or How to Enjoy Your Day 105
The Pig House 106
Siri 107
Garage Sales 108
Private Doors and Chalk-Drawn Squares 109
Saved in America 110
Maybe 111
Art 112
Blowing Bubbles 113

PART II

TRAVELING

FLIGHT

Seat 24B 119
Waste Receptacles 120
Sweeping in Dubai 121
Flight to Shanghai 122
Flight to Kenya 123
Blank Verse 125
In Flight 126
Flight of Fancy 127

CHINA

Suzhou Teacher Training: 3 Haiku 131
Rain Falls from Sky Like Blessings 132
Subway to Yushan Lu 133

Eating Dumplings in Shanghai Airport 134
First Morning in Suzhou 135
The Color of Suzhou on a Sunday 136

EL SALVADOR

Tito Drives Trucks 139
Aguilleres on a Sunday Morning 140
Basketball in La Palma 141
Beautiful Cakes We Bought at the Market 142
On the Streets of San Salvador 143
Santa Ana Winds 144

MALAYSIA

Gomantong Cave 147
A Malaysian Countryside 148
Fresh Fish from the Sulu Sea 149
View from a Mountaintop in Sapulut 150
Journey to Kudat I 151
Journey to Kudat II 152

KENYA

Leaving Kenya 155
Perspective 156
Offering (with apologies to Christina Rossetti) 157
Ambush 159
Every Day I Dream of Africa 160
Wishes Are Not Wings 162
So Funny, the Baboon 163
Circle of Life on Maasai Mara 164
Rain over Ndondori Hills 165
Buying Honey in Marigat 166
Centre of Hope – Kibera, Kenya 167
Kibera Samosas 168

Journey to Maasai Mara 169
Journey to Komolion 170
Balloon Safari 171
Amboseli 172
Baboon at Fig Tree 173
School Girl in Nairobi 174
Playing with Monkeys at Amboseli 175
African Rains 176
Heat of the Day 177
Elephant Challenge 178

COLORADO

Settlers Loop 181
Bat of Darkness 183
Mountain High 185
Morning at Hawley Court 187

THE SOUTH

Wooded Secret 191
Off Highway 106 192
Butler County 59 193
Summer Haiku 194
Sounds of the South 195
Jogging with Jack 196
Picking Kumquats on New Year's Eve 197

Part I

Seasons

NATURE

Abundance

When I pluck the grapes
from the vine,
a bit of pulp always
remains on the stem.
Just enough for the birds
in my yard to have a snack.
Not much is better than warm,
sun-kissed grapes picked fresh
from the arbor we built
to create a shade in the late afternoon sun.
Of course, when I'm not looking,
I think they eat the whole fruit.
That's why so many hulls lie
squashed and drying on the patio floor.
I don't begrudge them, though.
Bunches of green globes still hang.
How can they not be attracted
by the sweet juicy fruit
just as I am drawn by the bird song
every time I open my back door.

Fermata

A bird flies through the sky
in my backyard this afternoon
while I water plants in the garden
and two men on the roof next-door
hammer shingles in the blazing sun.
The words in my head keep pressing
against my eyelids.
Sun rays glisten like diamonds
coming from the water hose
before they land on the soil
beneath the eggplant and moisten
for a moment the dry soil
so that it bubbles
like little fish mouths
gasping for food.
A light breeze cools
the sweat on my forehead
just in time to keep me
outside a few minutes longer.
Oh, days of summer,
meant to slow my pulse
and make me notice.

Approaching Storm

The wind crescendos gradually,
forcing loose fence boards
to creak like dry bones
while the brittle leaves of the grape vine
blow in the hot air.
A few solitary birds chirp anxiously.
Somewhere a neighbor's dog barks incessantly.
A blue sky – intense with swirling clouds –
canvases the fuschia crepe myrtles and
dreamsicle orange trumpet vines.
Lavender periwinkles,
delicate pink, yellow-throated moss roses, and
purple velvet bachelor buttons
dance in protest against the approaching storm.
Bold-red begonias posture arrogantly
from their position in the rich soil.
Squirrels scatter as drops of rain
fall like pellets and pierce the summer stillness.

Change of Seasons

Only the undeveloped grapes remain on the vine;
the time has passed for them to ripen.
Early in the summer the deep purple
globes of sweetness were gathered
in bunches and eaten or left on the high branches,
too far to reach even with a ladder.
Ah, the satisfaction of potential realized:
of picking the fleshy fruit and
crunching the skin to release the warm juice.
But the immature ones stubbornly
cling to their branches, refusing to grow.
Soon the change of seasons
will force them to dry up or
fall to the ground below where
they will be crushed by moving feet.

Stopping by Bluebonnets on a Sunday Morning

The sun was not fully present
as I ran quickly past
my still sleeping neighbors early this morning.

A paper, rolled and patient,
lay ignored on the driveway.
White, fluffy heads wagged – right to left to right –
incessantly barking, pleading
for attention, for food, for freedom.

I anticipated their presence before I turned the corner –
a few stray blossoms haphazardly emerged beside the wooden fence –
teasing, foreshadowing the color to come.

My feet slowed – they stopped, really,
to take in the breadth of the vision:
rows of bluebonnets edged the length of the house,
mingled with the green,
their brilliant blue texture stacked like teardrops on a single stem,
a residential pasture of breathtaking beauty.

We have our unwritten boundaries here, in our concrete woods,
so I stood from a respectful distance and only imagined
sinking my nose into the lot of them.

Papa's Scuppernongs

August again and the scuppernong vines
    stretch four long rows,
      heavy with the ripening fruit.

Early morning, I walk eagerly
through the dewey grass –
    moisture soaks my sneakers –
to pick my pre-breakfast snack.

Even in the heat of the day,
    I am drawn to the warm sweetness.

With humidity wetting my brow and
    dripping down my neck,
I stand among the leaves –
    half shine in the blazing sun;
    half rest beneath an ancient pecan tree.

I reach my hand to pick a golden sphere, and
    push it into my mouth.
I bite down and pop the tough skin
    with my teeth.
Warm liquid flows over my tongue.
I spit out the seeds and skin and
    chew the slimy pulp.

I dodge a few wasps, and
by the time I get my fill,
    sweat stings my eyes,
      my shirt is drenched, and
I am ready to return to the comfort of the porch swing.

Meet Me in St. Louis at Park Avenue

I'll be sitting in the garden
beneath a fragrant magnolia tree.

A ruby-red Macaw with rainbow wings
perches on the top of my swing,
preening its feathers and studying me.

Its beak rests criss cross,
top lip over bottom,
as he inches closer toward me.

Placing his talons in his mouth,
he cleans them as a little
child would chew its nails.

We share the afternoon – silently, comfortably-
until a single turquoise feather
floats through the air and
lands at my feet.

I pick up this unsolicited gift and
place it in my book just as the bird
returns to the security of his tree branch.

Blackberry Picking

Early this morning we ride the Gator
to the backfield to pick blackberries.
The first few make a thump,
hitting the bottom of the white, plastic bucket
until soon there is enough to complete
our breakfast of grits, eggs, and
cold fish left from last night's supper.
Rounding a corner, we startle rabbits
and watch them hop across the trail in front of us.
We pass the pond where a large moccasin
is easily spotted, its head bobbing just above
the surface as it glides smoothly
into fallen tree branches floating
against the muddy bank.
We breathe a soft, fresh breeze
in the blue, cloudless sky just as
a large crane swoops down above the pond
and scoops a snake with his feet,
dangling it in the air and
flying majestically out of sight.

Loss

Mourning on Nanny's Porch

I am enveloped in grief
as dense and choking as
this early morning fog
that obscures the view
of everything beyond
the scuppernong vines
and peach trees.
It drips from my soul
like dew from
the pecan trees
and hanging ferns.
No sun shines
this early morning --
only a dim haze of light
glows through the branches.
Pomegranates hang
overripe and heavy.
Figs the birds left
lie rotting beneath the tree.
Ugly, the cat,
scrubs her bony neck
against my muddy,
gray tennis shoes.

Streetlights

come on in the orange dusk of evening,
pale blue sky striped with pink sun
reflects through the bare branches
onto the maze-colored grass
dotted with dried leaves
in this late February.
The air smells like copper and ashen memory.
Birdsong in my ear weighs
on my heart like a drum.

Cleaning Your Closet

I cleaned out your closet today.
I could not sort through your lives
in the moonlight.
I had to wait till morning
when the sun peeped its hopeful face
past the stardust and false promises of darkness.
At night the masks come off and
the pain feels raw and real.
At night the bandages are gone and
you discover the wounds have not healed.
So today I tossed your faded T-shirts and
holey socks in the garbage.
I placed your photos face down
in a crumpled manila folder.
I shredded your forgiven bills
and blank bank statements.
I bundled up your letters
and tied a yellow ribbon around them.
Yes. You went to war,
but the battles were of your choosing –
ones you did not fight
until too late.

Zippy Doodle

When you shook your head excitedly
from side to side and barked for a treat,
you had no idea that this was your last
morning in my life.
No more will you turn to greet
me with shiny, brown eyes
wide open in trust.
No more will you rest your
head on the back of the couch
and watch me in the kitchen.
Never again will you lie on the
warm patio floor while I
grade papers beside you.
You will not "fall down" so I
can kiss your tummy or run hide
under the dining room chair
until I pull you out in laughter.
You will no longer press your
warm body against my leg
as I read in my early morning chair.
You will not sing with joy and dance
around the living room
while someone plays the piano.
You will not sniff the shoes of friends
who come to visit nor wait impatiently for them to
acknowledge you with an affectionate touch.
Nor will you scrounge under the table,
hoping for a crumb to drop.
But you will lie under the forget-me-nots
planted on your grave in the late afternoon –
soft, blue reminders of the love you gave.

Caught Between Two Griefs

I arrived to see my dying father
on the eve of the death
of my country as I have known it.
The two passings, one to a brighter day,
the other to a darker place.
One moving ahead,
the other moving backward
to a time of fear, racism,
discrimination, and oppression.
Both occasions a letting go,
a loss of what was already "great."
I feel caught in a warp of unreality
on the eve of a tragic reality show,
and those that wait on the other side of this day:
hosts of angels and the arms of God
for the soul of my father;
greedy, egocentric hearts,
and small minds for the soul of my country.

As You Lay Dying

I kissed your cheek, paper thin
and soft as newborn skin,
your gray hair longer
than I've ever seen,
your raspy breath
in spurts and pauses
beneath the white t-shirt
split for ease of access,
your faint heart
barely raising the fabric
over your now bony shoulders.
Arthritic hands like paws
reach for sheet or air
or something visible to your eyes only
that see the other side
more clearly than
those of us you leave behind.
"I want to go home,"
you say, and I don't know
which home you mean
so I read scripture,
play the treble clef of old hymns,
and give you sips of water from a straw.
I tell you I love you
and ask if you know
I'm beside you.
I pick your last peppers,
show you the last tomatoes
you'll ever grow,
and break with you the bread
of homemade, buttered biscuits,
a kind of last supper until
you feast at eternity's table.

Song 88

Before I close the door and drive away,
I want to see your back stooped over your cane,
your left hand on the railing the Peavy boys built,
thin gray hair never altered from the crewcut
of Air Force days,
the melancholy half-smile of a goodbye.
I want to walk
in your garden
of potted pepper plants,
bright red tomatoes,
and yellow 4 o'clock's –
or ride with you
up the road to the neighbor's patch
where we'll pick watermelons and
wipe the dirt off before laying them
on the newspaper in the backseat.
Then we'll share
an episode, or two,
of *Walker, Texas Ranger*
at full volume
while Mama sits in her recliner
sporting bright orange earplugs.
We'll end the evening
with a game
of Shanghai Rummy,
which you will win -- because you almost always do.
After the evening news,
we'll all go to bed,
and soon I'll hear,
"Ken, Lord have mercy!"
and the vigorous shaking of a top sheet
as laughter peals from your bedroom.

The Power of a Smile

Leaves rustle like brittle paper
when my shoes scatter
the pile gathered by the soft wind
this late fall afternoon.
The sun reflects off the windshield of the school bus;
in the glare I fancy your face in the glass,
the power of a wise, friendly smile.
I think your hand reaches out the window to wave.
Your battered heart held love enough
for those of us with fleeting concerns.
Now your days here are past,
but I will listen for you
in the sounds of music,
the voice of a stranger,
the motor of a school bus every afternoon.

Slaughter of Innocents

Laughter of children riding bikes past my window
flows in waves of sound, then ebbs,
reminding me of what was
only a short time ago
when soft peace and bright innocence took residence here.

With no apparent foreshadowing, no transition,
the darkness creeped in while we slept
– like Grendel on a premeditated rampage –
dispelling the warmth and slaughtering the innocents.

Was it the careless glance at the glitz and glamor of the world
that left the hall unguarded?
Was it the word thoughtlessly spoken? The lie flippantly told?
Was it the stroke of false love? The wafting scent of instant pleasure?
The flavor of the forbidden?

This early morning hour – the house still asleep –
fear fogs the future, threatening to dismiss trust,
irretrievably this time.

A Thin Line

There is a thin line between
    light and darkness,
        pleasure and pain,
            joy and sorrow,
                life and death.

We all walk the tightrope in this realm
more than it ever occurs to us to realize.

Tonight you crossed the line.
You held on to dear life as long as you could;
then with family gathered,
    giving permission to let go,
you did.

As the tears flowed,
they came to take your body –
    leaving a full life,
        an empty house, and
           years of memories.

UNNOTICED

My neighbor died last week,
a private woman who seldom spoke.
Occasionally, she shuffled to the mailbox,
    pulled weeds from her flower bed,
        drove away in her long, white van
           wearing designer clothes and salon hair.

Once her dog barked all night;
    without her hearing aids, she heard no sound,
    not even my knock on her door at 2 A.M.
Once I baked her bread.
Once she brought us cookies.

My neighbor died without my notice –
    winter leaves gathered around her dark door,
        windows curtain-drawn,
           a newspaper abandoned on her
driveway, and
I never noticed.

We live in protected spaces –
    safe, secure homes and private fences –
and seldom notice.

VISITATION

Behind my mask and plastic gloves,
I watch the nurses switch your IV bags and
wait in the silence.

Only our eyes touch as we say goodbye;
we must keep our distance.
We leave you sitting in the chair beneath the blanket,
face gaunt and breath shallow.

In the elevator, a young couple
holds a sack and
waits for the descent.

The door opens to the lobby;
an old man glances up from his paper
to see us leave the building.

Outside on the corner,
a woman holds her ipod and
loudly sings a Gospel melody.

We walk into the sunshine and
make our way to the car where we can escape;
but first I will linger in the gentle breeze
beneath the sturdy oaks and
remember this first day of autumn
which moves too quickly toward its end.

Empty Spaces

This morning I drove through your apartment complex,
past the spot where I used to see your car parked,
past the stairs where we carried boxes,
past the door where I laid your first welcome mat,
past the door where we tried to organize your life:
purchases of love
from dollar stores and garage sales.
Do you remember the estate sale
where we bought kitchenware and a mini Christmas tree?
Do you remember the pots and pans,
the microwave, the full length mirror?
The plates and matching bowls?
Do you remember the shower curtain
and the time I scrubbed mold off the bathroom vent?
The pottery bowl where I placed coins
for the washer you never used?
Now your space is empty like my heart;
my hope splashes against the windshield
like the tears falling down my cheeks.

Summer Fruit

I visited the grocery store today to buy summer fruit.
I found, instead, the auto aisle
where I imagined you standing before the buffing puff,
                              turtle wax, and
                                                    chamois cloth,
all lined neatly on the shelf.

As quickly as I saw you, you were gone.

Moments are funny that way:
        like the smudge on a car door,
        a fishing line in the lake,
        magic bubbles in the air . . .
once you notice them, someone wipes them away or
they vanish from view.

Finally, I walked to the produce section,
        put some cherries, peaches, and a mango in my cart, and
                went home alone.

The Garden

I walk into the garden
this morning,
the sun hot and bright.
My heart beats
through the soles
of my feet
into the dry soil
of this sacred space.
Massive heads of cabbage
transport me to a day
when I rode with you
to the vegetable patch
and forgot a moment
that you could not pull
the bounty from the ground.
So you hobbled with your cane
to the small hill
while I spread newspaper
in the open trunk.
Together we carried the fruit
of your neighbor's labor,
laying it carefully
before driving slowly home,
the August breeze blowing in our content faces.

You're gone now and only
memories connect us.

I Want to Buy You Pretty Things

I want to see your copper penny hair
shine in the Light of a sunny day,
to talk and laugh with abandon
in the hope of your choices,
to dream, to plan the future into being.
I want to buy you pretty things,
to drape your softness in gentle beauty,
to shower your soul with cleansing rain and
warm your heart till the passion,
lying dormant in the layers of the ages,
rises to the surface in glorious fire and life.

On Joy in the Morning

In the cool of morning before daybreak,
when all are sleeping and I am alone,
I lift my eyes to the dark, quiet sky.
I shake my fist and scream a voiceless, "Why?"
Too soon it comes, this life-consuming death,
to ravage, crush, and shamelessly destroy
overwhelming heart, and mind, and spirit
with fear, dread, grief, and a despairing loss.
Cold the hands that clasp my shrinking spirit.
Yet in my own deep, dark "night of the soul,"
a voice rises to turn my fear to peace,
a heart beats steady in uncertain days –
the sun, bright, shining, bursting forth with joy.
A purpose for the future tho' obscure.

NOT A DOOR

It takes bravery or naivete or stupidity
to walk up to the door that is not a door,
blinds hanging loose and broken
on a grimy window revealing the darkness within.
Below the door that is not a door,
leaves collect, thick from neglect,
a bag of charcoal and dusty grill wait, abandoned and unused.
The bell on the door that is not a door
makes no sound – we knock. Loudly.
The impact on the rotting wood
shakes the window panes.
"Oh, shit!" exclaims the running feet I do not recognize.
Eventually, she emerges –
not from the door that is not a door
but from the shadows of shrubbery grown wild and unrestrained
like the one in whose hands I place
a key and a slice of warm banana bread,
whose lips brush fleetingly across my aging cheek.

The Waiting Room

In the waiting room,
the air is thick with waiting –
waiting for kindness,
waiting for a smile,
waiting for "next,"
waiting for hope.
In the waiting,
the bodies are expectant
but hollow:
eyes recessed,
ears protruded from sunken flesh,
hair vanished or thin.
Most walk slowly or shuffle.
Above all – this room
is full of humanity:
temporal, sacred temples of flesh.

'Mid Tubes and Blankets

Within four walls where beep machines of
strange, ominous foreboding,
Love, O sweet Love, moves gracefully
among the family gathered there.
Redemption comes in many forms –
transformation, forgiveness –
not always spoken but acted,
often observable, distinct:
My daughter gently helps me bathe
with calm, confident hands;
my son anoints my feet with lotion,
moves his fingers with deep love.
My children talk and laugh freely –
together, together.
If I should die before I wake,
I have seen the hands of mercy,
I have felt the grace of God.

FAITH

ADVENT

Somewhere I have been waiting for you –
not so intentionally, I fear.

Christmas songs have been sung,
candles lit,
cookies baked,
presents exchanged.

In the colored lights
a shadow looms,
masking the potential
for light hearts and laughter.

Focused on the darkness
and afraid of the mystery,
I have sought easy answers
and quick fixes.

Yet in this melancholy time
of facing the future
remembering the past,
somehow you wait for me –
patiently,
intentionally.

Not Yet

On these two words
hope rests softly
like butterfly on flower petal;
velvet color holds our gaze.
Not yet.
We wait, we watch
for the flutter of angels' wings.
Sometimes too hard our stare,
our touch would press heavy,
could crush the fragile fellow.
Not yet.
We wait, we trust
the mystery wind.

Among the Ashes

Tonight I will sit in the discomfort of silence,
in the pain of ash and grit,
the stain of regret,
the ache of abandonment,
the rejection of betrayal,
the grief of loss,
the anguish of lingering memories.
I will sit in silence and enter into
the suffering of Christ.

Yahweh

For pain too raw for tears,
Yahweh.
For fear that stops my breath,
Yahweh.
For chattering voices in my head,
Yahweh.
For trust that shatters time and time again,
Yahweh.
Yahweh – the very breath of God.
For expressions unspeakable,
Yahweh.
For hope unquenchable,
Yahweh.
For battles undefeatable,
Yahweh.
For answers undeniable,
Yahweh.
For joy indescribable,
my heart cries *Yahweh*.
Yahweh – the very breath of God.

For This Moment

Thank you, Jesus, that at this moment in time,
life is beautiful and you are present.
You shine on days ahead bright with hope and promise –
your hand always guiding, leading.
You touch my heart with peace
in the midst of crisis and chaos.
You give stillness to the chattering mind,
possibility to the step toward transformation.
You give courage through friends
who walk this path with me.
You give beauty in the singing of the brilliant-colored birds,
the soft breeze on my skin.

Faint as a Frightened Bird

I should be shouting joyous celebrations
to the wide-opened space before me
with a sound so loud as to shake the stones,
to raise the sleeping heads from out their graves,
to shake dry bones to glorious life.
My voice is but still upon the hill,
the birds – they sing my praises,
the breeze stirs my heart, but not so deep my soul.
Once long ago I waited in this place
and lifted pleas to the high heaven.
So dim the voice returned I was not sure the source.
Only a desperate faith and drop of hope
kept alive the dreams
that dared to form.
Now trust rises
faint as a frightened bird,
not sure where to land or for how long.

Dust

Tonight I am dust
falling from clouded skies,
settling loosely
on cattle shoulders
and tombstone grasses.
I am carried by wind
to city streets
and rushing people,
to sidewalks
and park benches,
to skyscraper windows
and truck beds,
to creek and hillside,
field and farm.
Blow, Wind, blow –
carry me softly –
like bird wing feathers –
to eyes that see my source,
to bowed, humble hearts,
to the souls of all who wait.

Before the Dawn

Before the dawn breaks,
before the sun wakes,
I will trust you.
Before the clouds part,
Before I lift my heart,
I will trust you.
Before the empty tomb,
Before the rising gloom,
I will trust you,
and I will thank you
for the light
that will come
in the darkness —
for truth and for resurrection.

Baraka za Mungu

Alasiri, nimechoka
uzito mila, maisha.
Haraka, haraka haina baraka.
Hapana saa
kutafakari,
hapana saa
kuangalia
wakati wa jua mahiri
rangi za
zambarau, samawati,
waridi na machungwa,
kama moto mwitu mbinguni,
kama nishati na ajabu,
kama baraka za Mungu.

(translation)
Blessings of God

Late afternoon, the weary weight
of culture, life presses.
Hurry, hurry has no blessing.
No time for contemplating,
no time for looking
at vibrant sunsets
in colors of
purple, blue,
pink and orange,
like wild fire in the sky,
like energy and wonder,
like the blessings of God.

Sometimes We Wait

Sometimes we wait
a step short of long enough,
only half expecting
> our worries to dispel,
> our prayers to be answered,
> our hearts to be filled.

We turn away blinded by the world in our eyes,
before grace has a chance to walk in.
> Be still and know.

Inhale God's peace in the wind
breathing into our souls
cool refreshment and rest.
> Be still and wait.

See God hold out
a sweet comb of honey,
dripping with mercy and blessings.
> Be still and taste.

Hear now God's song of
joy to the world,
sounding from the open-beaked throats of birds.
> Be still and listen.

BLESSING

Children gather for the blessing
poured out from lips of those
who love, who know what waits.
Hands extend, the prayer washing over all.
A child strays, runs from the
blessing, but the Spirit blows
and follows – beyond the house
of praise and security to the world beyond.
Beyond these walls Love pursues,
unwilling though we are to accept.
We turn our faces to the dark
but Christ walks and suffers with us,
calling us to the light.
His blood covers us and washes us –
cleansing, healing, restoring.

BREATH OF GOD

In the dewey mist of morning,
when the day has just begun,
through the rhythm of our living
all of us can serve as one.

In the bustle of the midday
life and work are all around.
As we run the race before us,
tender mercies can be found.

In the hazy hush of evening,
fading light sifts through the leaves
and falls softly on creation
gracing all with time to breathe.

The breath of God stills the heart
and brings peace and rest.

MEMORY

POOL IN DECATUR

Today I sit beside the pool.
Tree branches hang
over the edge
dropping blossoms and leaves
onto the ripples of the water.
It's cool here. And peaceful.
And I can find Jesus
here just fine,
thank you very much.
So I rise from
my fuzzy pink towel
and splash into the crisp water
while the sun shines
on my copper hair.
Beneath the surface
is silence –
no birds, no words, no music,
only the purr of the pool motor
and my own thoughts
caught on the thin line
between sound and silence.
Maybe someone somewhere
is singing a song for me.
Maybe I will hear it someday.

Corner of Lee and 35

Today you stand
at the corner
of Irving Lee and 35,
three duffel bags
slung over your shoulder.
Your baseball cap covers
a haircut just beginning
to grow out,
shoulders and arms
still bear the cut
of gym visits,
even your shoes
would pass muster.
How long have you been
standing there —
cardboard sign,
ignored, beside you?
You pace.
Still in denial, aren't you?
Can't believe yourself how
you've dropped so far.
Is that why
I don't make eye contact?
Am I afraid I'll *see* you,
See *myself*?
Am I afraid I'll step
over the invisible line
separating us?

Worry Stories

Worry stories keep
weaving in my mind
like spider webs
that form at dawn
and trap my head
when I walk out
the front door to face
a new day.
All I want is to be free
of the tangled mess
and walk forward,
undistracted and unimpeded.
The plot is always the same:
Two roads diverged
in a wood
and you took the
road less traveled.
But there's no rising action;
only falling,
       falling,
              falling. . . .
Maybe my greatest fear
is that as way
leads on to way,
you will never turn back.

Life in the Shadows

Like Pandora, you lifted the lid.
The sharp-winged being slid in
through a sliver of space,
lured by your curiosity.
He flew around defiantly,
sharp edges pricking the skin of your innocence,
until, thickened by the ruthless jabs,
you lifted the closure higher and more creatures
flew in, overwhelming your consciousness,
snuffing out the fire of your passions,
smothering your dreams,
smoke from the dying embers
clouding your vision of a future.
Now you only wake in darkness,
living in the shade of your past,
but life in the shadows is no life at all.
Where's the hope for freedom
from the shackles of your sins?
Untie the blinds –
even a shaft of light will pierce
the darkness enough to banish the
evil into the corners where it will cower,
desperate and powerless in the presence of Light.

Broken Silence

Today I took a breath –

The sun shone in the crisp autumn sky,
soft winds blew grape leaves from the arbor onto the patio,
birds flitted from branch to feeder singing their melodies,
bread baked in the oven,
soup simmered on the stove,
music played on the kitchen radio.

Without warning, the phone rang –

Suddenly, clouds rolled in,
gutters banged the walls of the house as winds increased,
the birds quieted.

Words provoking anger
spoke injustice against my child.
No forum to scream of
the ignore-ance of one unchosen,
the attempt not made,
the heart broken –
the slight,
the cold eye turned to another.

The stage empty now,
dust settles on the spaces once filled
with sweet, warm voices and
hopeful hearts.
Only the music of silence echoes in the barren hall.

Valley and Shadows

I live in what I imagine to be your shadows,
    in what I suppose are your valleys.
I long to pull you out and set you on a higher plane,
    away from your darkness,
    away from your pain.

By dwelling in your struggle,
    I sink to valleys of my own design and
give in to a self which controls
    neither choices nor consequences.

I forget to trust,
        to lean,
            to wait,
                to learn.

I forget
    that shadows offer shade,
    that shadows presuppose light,
    that valleys prepare us to recognize mountains.

SCRIPTWRITER

It's not my play,
but I keep trying
to write the script.
None of the characters
will read it anyway.
Besides, this is real-life drama.
You can't make this stuff up and tie it with a pretty bow.
So I make up dialogue
in my head and rehearse
it late at night when
I should be sleeping.
When I run out of ideas,
I lay the words
on the table
until morning when
I pick them up again.

Sharp Memories

Tonight we sit
at the table
long after our meal
is finished.
I lean my head
to avoid the glare
of setting sun
shining through
the blind slats
as we talk
of sharp memories
until our hearts bleed.
Time has flowed over
the painful places
like the river Lethe,
but sometimes
the past rises,
demanding to sit awhile
and be remembered.

Starbucks Run

My hand pushes open the library doors
where students chat softly
or hover heads over books.
A voice booms, *mi madre!*
as the shiny black hair and
dimpled cheeks walk toward me.
We run to the car and start the motor
while you toss your backpack behind us.
With laughter and music
we reach our destination,
stopping occasionally to video some antic.
Eight bucks easily run from my card
into the register where the barista
turns to pour latte into familiar cups.
Are we trying to out-run time,
refusing to count the last
of the 56 Tuesdays and Thursdays since September?
We will not label these moments as an end
but will let them float as memory clouds
that come to us softly and with joy.

The Longing

This afternoon I stand in my grandmother's kitchen
in front of the Formica-topped table
with yellow plastic cushions.
The faint scent of gas rises from her cooktop,
the Frigidaire hums a low tune,
an empty coffee cup sits in the sink,
sticky residue around the edge
from the toast my grandfather dipped
in the steaming liquid last night before bed.
Stale biscuits, left over from breakfast,
wait in the chipped saucer,
a crumbly afternoon snack for the adults
when they wake from mid-afternoon naps
about the same time my sisters and I beg
for bowls of vanilla ice milk before running
outside to play "make believe"
and cook dinner with mimosa fronds.
We slam the rickety screen door,
leaving all but memories behind us.

Time

The Bon Fire

Hot dogs blister and marshmallows char
on the makeshift roasting spears
plunged into the glowing embers
of the bon fire where –
for our winter ritual –
we have hauled meat and buns,
chips and drinks, and
fixings for s'mores
to the edge of the wood
before the dancing fire
built by former children
who earlier gathered the sticks and brush
to prepare the offering
for the sake of love.
The night will shine
with celebration of color and sound, and
sizzling sticks will draw smoky circles in the air.
Too soon the coals cool and all scatter
to the fabricated warmth of the house
while chill winds plink
wind chimes on the porch and
distant dogs bark.

Running South

Running south
out of the driveway
onto Cedar Road
out of the dark house
with TV blaring
at full volume,
curtains closed
against the day,
old folks planted
in recliners--
their bottoms growing roots in the cushions,
I run away
from the grains
of sand that fly
into my shoes
between my feet
and running socks,
away from the dark
stillness of age,
away from a small world
of small perspectives
in small words
in small minds.
I run away from sedentary, debilitating age,
away from stiff joints, weak limbs, soft bellies.
I push up the steep hill,
through the fog
of negative thoughts,
past the drenching humidity of complaining criticism,
the barren branches of ingratitude.
Jack runs with me, too.
His tongue hangs out of his parted, drooling lips,
and he smiles at our shared escape.

My Life Will Go On

My emotions stick to me this moist day
clogging my pores,
oppressing my breath,
clouding memories of the past
beneath a fog of unknowing,
drabbing the bright hopes for tomorrow.
But life goes on.
I run past the Dogspaw Mobile Grooming truck
and the Belle Window Cleaning sign,
for sale here,
sold there.
Life goes on.
The school bus passes,
the birds sing,
the squirrels eat nuts together
behind the parked car.
Life goes on.
I'll take you hangers and your check,
a can of beans, a wing and a prayer.
But then I'll drive away
because you have to choose to fly,
because my life will go on.

They May Never Be Remembered

If someone doesn't write them down,
they may never be remembered –
these moments when the blinker
on the airport shuttle
sounds *click, click, click, click*
or the voice on the speaker
asks *Does anyone have a key to the
White Ford parked in Lot D?*
Someone may not remember the wide-eyed
wonder on the face of the young
man holding the hockey stick,
raising his duffle bag impatiently
each time the bus slows or
the middle-aged couple who
anticipates their stop
with practiced patience,
realizing departure places them
one step closer
to the end of their journey.

CRACKING INNOCENCE

When I was twelve,
I painted my nails lilac
to match the new dotted Swiss dress
my mother made for me to wear to the
Saturday daycare at Haine's Furniture store
where she worked a 6-day week
to bring home enough money
for more than frozen pot pies for dinner.
All morning I watched other children
from my corner of the playroom
until a girl my age invited me to follow her.
As soon as she lit her cigarette,
I fled with fear and trembling
to the perceived safety
of my mother's workspace,
still afraid of cracking my own youthful innocence
as I first remembered doing years before
when I entered our barn and ran smack into the middle of
a lie.
When lunchtime came, my mother and I
left the store to eat hamburgers and fries
while Roberta Flack sang "Killing Me Softly"
on the restaurant's tabletop radio.

She Sent You Away to Pick Strawberries

She sent you away to pick strawberries early this morning
in the wild woods behind your summer cabin.
The pail's thin, silver handle rested in your bony fingers
as you shuffled out of the kitchen,
the unhinged screen slamming against the back door.

Before long, you returned, lost face pale and confused,
shirt drenched in sweat as if from hard labor,
breath coming in quick, deep gulps.

Gently, she took the container from your hand and placed it on the table
where you sat to drink cool water.
She wiped your brow with a cloth
while you set the empty glass beside the empty pail
and closed your eyes.

Clay Pot

This restaurant has fed
me for years,
first with a young family –
children who refused all
but noodles and French butter –
then a quick tea-to-go
of mysterious roots simmering
in a steaming pot
behind the counter;
lunches with friends, colleagues –
meetings of import and
casual chatter,
where we shared laughter
and empty stomachs,
stories and struggles;
a colorful, oxymoronic bathroom
and floor tables
where lounging diners
could remove shoes and custom
to sit for a few.
We watched your children grow –
and you, ours,
from baby carrier
to first car parked outside.
Time has floated
through bowls of pho
and plates of fresh spring rolls,
the transport of food
to a land beyond the now
that gives courage and hope
to walk out the door
and carry on.

In the Meantime

Sometimes, in the meantime,
you meet a friend for lunch or breakfast
and she listens to your heart breaking,
picks up the pieces,
and holds them in her hands.
Sometimes, in the meantime,
you take the memories out of the attic
and sell them in a garage sale
because they're too painful to keep.
Sometimes, in the meantime,
you wake up at 3 A.M.
and go to the window
just to be sure she's safe
and then turn on the light
to dispel the darkness – literally –
because that's the only switch
you can control.
Sometimes, in the meantime,
you choose beauty because
at this time life can be mean
and ugly and all you can do is wait
and pray and hope and trust.

Biscuits and Hot Coffee

In those years
we would stand
by the fire
in our robes and
wait for the chill
of dawn to melt,
wait for the laughter
of children to rise
in this stale, old house,
wait for the smell
of buttery biscuits
and hot coffee,
wait for family
to gather round the table
and make precious memories.

Horseflies and Butterflies

For years I've run
down Blueberry Lane
avoiding rocks and mud,
horseflies, gnats, and
wandering hunting dogs.
I've watched butterflies
and deer and listened
to crows and mourning doves
and wild turkeys.
I've stopped by Beaver Dam
and listened to water
rush over the twigs and branches.
I've listened to thunder clouds
rolling in a summer storm.
I've picked blueberries,
honeysuckle, and pinecones.
I've wiped away sweat
from August suns
and Alabama humidity.
But most of all,
I've breathed deeply
of time and hope
and peace.
For this moment,
I've silenced all
sounds but nature.
I've ignored all obstacles
but those beneath my feet.
I've fixed my eyes on
that which brings me joy.
And I've dreamed dreams
that will carry me
beyond this red clay earth.

Numbered Sunrises

What if this pain
means my sunrises
are numbered,
that I won't see
bluebonnets next year
or Indian paintbrush,
that I won't lean
against sun-warmed bricks
or listen to birds
from my patio,
that I won't taste
gingerbread lattes in autumn
or smell pumpkin cookies baking?
What if I can't see
your smile or
hold your hand
or watch the sun set
in the massive Texas sky?

Noticing Time

Time flies like the quick wind
of a late March afternoon —
persistent, intent on being noticed.
In the calm sun
I listen to
the dried leaves
dancing on the driveway,
the busy birds
scratching for seeds
in the backyard feeder,
the dog next door
barking hello
as my neighbor
returns for the evening.

Mending Fences

You spent the morning
mending fences
beside the pine trees,
stopping only to drink water
and listen to wild turkeys
in the distance.
In the afternoon,
you spread pine straw
in the flowerbeds,
whose budding color
shows signs of spring.
A neighbor drives up
on his four wheeler,
engaging you with
a friendly chat.
Later, as twilight falls,
you take the gator
to the back field
and watch for deer.
Thirty-five you see that evening.
Soon, you return
to sit around a table
built with your own hands,
sharing catfish
and wisdom stories –
shoring up warm memories
for tomorrow's work.

Master Betrayer

Every morning for 30 years
William Howard and Roseanne
drive up late morning
in their pickup truck
and return to the house
from whence they came.
I never noticed till today
what time has taken.
Now an old man,
William emerges with cane
and obvious limp.
He is not the only change:
the pine trees have been clearcut,
the path to the blueberry patch
has been barred with a "closed" sign,
most of the houses on Cedar Road
have been abandoned and ignored.
Even my mother's house
is closed for business
except for a few days each season.
Time, you Master Betrayer,
what pleasure take you in hasty robbery?

Magnolias and Blue Bottles

On cloudy days when raindrops
blur the window panes
and the cold wind
keeps you closed inside,
remember the sunny mornings
of birdsong and blooming
camellias and azaleas
and scented magnolias.
When just two share
cups of tea in the glow
of a television screen
and the only sound
is soft snowfall and
the tinkle of cup on saucer,
remember the blaze
of a roaring bonfire,
the laughter of children
and barking dogs,
the smell of hot coffee.
When you place folded sweaters
and thrift store treasures
on your bedroom shelves,
remember baskets hanging
from kitchen ceiling,
blue bottles on cabinet ledges
and willow figurines
above the mantle.
When you feel the pangs
of loneliness,
remember visits from Willodene,
Ouida and Clarice,
from William Howard and Buddy.

You are not forgotten,
you are loved.
Another day you will return;
you will hear the tire
on gravel driveway,
and when you place your head
upon your pillow,
may you dream
of stored memories
and feel gentle arms
of peace surround you

Hotwheels and Invitations

Once you sat on the floor,
legs outstretched,
blocks and hotwheels between.
A Daniel Boone cap on your head,
you stood in front of the TV
in your little shorts and tank top,
skinny legs and arms
poised to attack the bad guys
or dance excitedly to the theme music.
Eyes shining, head back in laughter or song,
your presence created a warmth and joy to all around.
This afternoon you sit –
same place, same posture –
surrounded by neat stacks of graduation invitations
that mark an end.
Your smiles more fleeting,
your laughter occasional.
The future looms heavy and near.
You are ready.

Homeworker

His smooth, tanned fingers hold the green pencil and
move it confidently across the paper.

For hours now he's worked –
      writing,
            reading,
                   completing what is asked.

He stops briefly to gulp a glass of water,
ice cubes reflecting the kitchen's light.

He wipes his mouth and returns to the task.

Only once he looks up,
      sighing as he imagines the ball in his hand,
         hitting the pavement and
              sailing into the basket.

Early Years Revisited

Tonight we sleep in a hotel,
twenty minutes from the house
where we once lived.

The trees were young then –
      as were we.
The red door and blue shutters welcomed us.

The leaves surprised us each fall
      with vibrant color.
Leaving an apple pie in the oven,
      we took a walk in the early evening.
Weekends held adventures to small towns and the countryside.

We return briefly to roads
      which once led us to familiar people and places
      where we built a life and
      began a family.

We have aged –
      time has wrinkled our faces,
      stooped our shoulders,
      dimmed our sight, and
      thinned our hair.

Our children
will soon leave us
to make memories of their own.

Somebody's Little Boy

You're somebody's little boy all grown up.
Yesterday you reached your arms to be carried.
You ran circles around me in the back yard,
where we flew the see saw to New York City,
your black hair shining in the sunlight,
your laughter floating in the air like bubbles.
We rode to the church where you would "eat your breakfast all,"
and I would release your small hand to the care of another.
Now the drum beats rhythms in the den,
your fingers sail across the keys in the living room,
your voice thunders rich notes through the house.
Sometimes you grab your keys and run out the door
because you have places to be and people to see.
But sometimes you whisk me up,
rush me through the house,
toss me on the couch,
then walk away still carrying my heart.

Copper Strand

A most perfect strand of copper hair
floats onto my lap
when I open my window
parked as I am beside a graveside
in the Valley Mills Cemetery.
I don't know why I stop
except for the quiet unknowing,
the silent answers to Why? How?
The sheen of color dances in the sun –
"The Dazzler," we once said about a
hotel in Argentina where you,
perhaps for the first time,
learned the power of love
in a city cemetery
for the has been's and did nothing's.
I lift the lock to the light –
reds and blond fade
into the blandness of brown –
as, caught by the wind,
it disappears to lie among the tombstone grasses.

RELATIONSHIPS

Anniversary

Twenty-eight years – but who's counting?
Sometimes we're still eighteen, and
our life together is just beginning.
Wasn't it last night we sat on my parents' porch swing and
dreamed of the future?
Only yesterday afternoon we picnicked on the golf course?
Yesterday morning you brought me flowers
from a neighbor's yard?
But now our daughter is seventeen – only a year younger
than we were.
Breaking my reverie, she comes outside now
to water the thirsty plants while
you stand in the kitchen and make peanut butter.

In the Garden

I come to the garden alone while
you check email in Lafayette Square.

Mixing business with anniversary,
we chose to leave our children yesterday and
fly away.

Awaking early this morning,
I watched you sleeping –
your body tangled among the sheets,
your breath measured by whole rests.

I left you to sit in the shade of a magnolia tree,
to listen to the chirping of St. Louis birds and
the water fountains in this lovely garden.

Hydrangeas and hostas surround me,
the cool breeze surprises my summer skin.

A curious squirrel sneaks up behind my swing and
watches the pen hesitate across the paper.

By now, my coffee has chilled in the cup, so
I move to the sunshine of the patio and
wait for you.

Everybody's Got a Little Hot Pink Toe Polish in 'Em!

After a 3 mile run and a cup of coffee at 6 A.M.,
my dog watches me spread homemade peanut butter and
drip Papa's honey on my breakfast toast;
      she knows I'll let her lick my finger.
I am a thoughtful pet owner.

Then I tackle dirty clothes: *Where'd that stain come from?*
      floors: *Who dropped this sticky mess?*
      toilets: *What is that black stuff?*
I am a responsible mother.

This afternoon I update my fall syllabi and
dream of ways to engage my students,
to equip and empower them to make a difference.
I am a prepared teacher.

Tonight I serve crusted Dijon salmon and
grilled asparagus on a candle-lit, linen-covered table
because the kids are not home.
I am a loving wife.

Tomorrow I'll let the summer sun kiss my skin
while I sit on the patio, drink Topo Chico, and read a novel –
just for fun.
Then I'll go to Mi Nail Spa and choose hot pink polish.

Under the Hackberry

We parked the car under the hackberry tree
beside the farmhouse where we stayed
for three days – an escape from city life.
The night was black as pitch,
not even stars welcomed us,
so we used the artificial light of the phone
to make our way without tripping
on a snake or a broken tree branch.
Other than a few necessities,
all I carried inside were some
memories, obligations, and worries,
placing them in neat stacks so I could
lay my eyes on them – if not my heart –
each time I passed through the room.
When the morn dawned,
I greeted the day in sun salutation
and tried to release the trappings in my mind
so I could breathe awhile.
I walked on the rocky path as far as the windmill,
purple and yellow flowers peeping
above the pasture grasses. Lovely.
Sky blue and crystal clear.
In the distance a manure spreader
fertilizes pasture lands for cattle feed.
In the heat of day and cool of evening,
the smell wafted in our open windows.
Blessed nourishment – seeping into
the ground and our noses.
As the sun set, hills of cattle
grazed as peacefully as wildebeest
on an African plain,
bodies lobbing slowly forward,

heads hanging low.
Inside we ate our dinner and
crated our puppy for the night.
We made our way upstairs
as crickets and cicadas chirped a lullaby.

The Farmhouse

The sun was already setting
as we drove toward the
barren landscape west of Waco
on Friday afternoon.
Our destination: the farmhouse in Hamilton,
where we've gone many times now --
a reprieve from the noise of traffic,
to-do lists, and social obligations.
We stop at a Mexican restaurant in Clifton
and remember the last time
we ate there -- 2013.
We were headed back
to Waco. Memories.
When we park beside
the familiar Hackberry tree,
we unload by car light.
As we raise the windows
to let in the breeze,
dried bugs and cobwebs disintegrate
into powder on the ledge.
A dead mouse lies in the middle
of the bedroom floor as I enter.
A menacing spider
crawls across the ceiling
above the toilet.
We settle in bed
between open windows that offer
a generous cross flow of air.
In the middle of the night
we are serenaded by the howl
of a coyote pack.

Afternoons and Coffeespoons

Drinking a gingerbread latte
on a sunny winter afternoon
at Starbucks, she approached me —
hair a shade of cotton candy.
"Your pants are the color of springtime,"
she said through lips of pink fairy glitter.
In the afternoons we gather
in this coffee commune
with our coffee spoons
with our books and conversation
to avoid the lonely spaces.
We remember what was
or imagine what could be.
Max sits each week and sketches faces;
once he drew my daughter.
She took the paper home
to preserve under her mattress.
Dottie shows up every afternoon
and desperately searches for eye contact
so she can feed her voracious
appetite for connection.
I come to grade papers or watch people,
to create stories of their lives,
to step out of mine.
I carry them with me, even so –
the memories, the pain and joy of it all.

The 5th Afternoon

This is the 5th afternoon
of the 30th spring break of our marriage.
We had planned to spend it
away from the rat race pace
of our academic lives.
We committed to ignore
the voices in our emails
and cells that try to speak
loudly enough to call us
away from time away.

We loaded up the car –
canned food, bread, peanuts,
books, paper, yoga mat, DVD's,
a few clothes –
and headed for the hills

Welcomed by a herd of cattle,
we crossed the livestock guard
and found the key under the doormat.
Bright sunflower dishes decorated
the breakfast room table
beside the cozy kitchen.
But the clouds were blocking the sun and
a cool rain was beginning to fall.

Maybe it was the rigid wicker sofa
that drove us to leave the next morning,
the beeping of the smoke alarm throughout the night,
the flicker of the proprietor's TV between the sunroom doors,
the whispering we were constrained to do.
Or maybe we needed a soft place to be,

a familiar, safe space
like the home we felt compelled to leave.
So now the birds are singing and the sun is shining on the warm patio.
The wind blows gently.

Woodway Park II

On a lazy sunny Wednesday afternoon,
we stopped to play disc golf
in a place you had discovered for yourself
but chose to share with me.
We flung the disks from our fingertips like heat waves of worry
into baskets that held on loosely,
dropping them to the ground again
where we picked them up and carried them with us.
At each station the disks grew lighter as we showered
the air with laughter and smiles.
I don't recall lengthy conversation
or deep thoughts spoken,
but I will always remember
the lake lapping onto the bank,
your strong arm curving the disk around a tree
and into the goal with only two tries,
your hand on my shoulder, briefly, as we walked back to the car.

One Day

I used to be so embarrassed,
standing beside our beat-up car
outside the restaurant
while my parents smoked,
cracked window patched with
duct tape, missing hubcaps.
The nicotine rush
would make them giddy,
and they would talk and talk.
My mother's greasy hair
hung in gray strands
down her back,
held loosely
by a rubber band taken
from the morning paper;
my father's white, stained t-shirt
stretched taut over his paunch.
I lowered my eyes in shame
but not before she saw
the fire in my eyes.
She with the nice dress,
the nice, nice shoes,
the kind smile.
Not before my mouth
formed the words,
"One day, one day . . . ."

Upon the Occasion of Your High School Graduation: June 1, 2012

March forward now with confidence into
a future of your own making. You've passed
through the halls of youth, sometimes distracted
by trivialities along the way.

You hold memories of a life already
full and rich with experiences and
opportunities that some never know, so
practice gratitude and joy. Seek truth and justice.

Listen. Embrace discontentment
from which often flower sacrifice, change,
and great gain. Pursue faith by asking hard
questions, and listen for unexpected,
simple answers – or no answers at all.

Look for hope in what lies ahead. Choose love
and kindness – we are all "the least of these."
Change your world through a life of service.

Evening in Calvert

Setting our bags on the B & B bed,
we walk into town in the late afternoon
to gape into store windows already closed.

Only The Wooden Spoon welcomes us,
so we enter a room, spacious yet empty,
until characters arrive to paint the scene with local color:

They sit alone and silent, an aged man and wife.
After bending to whisper in her ear,
he chooses from the menu for her and
places a napkin in her lap.
Occasionally, he gazes at her sadly
while she raises a fried shrimp
with trembling fingers to her slitted lips.

Meanwhile, an ordinary middle-aged woman –
surely someone's grandmother –
perches on a stool to sing, glancing up briefly from the mic and music
as her shy, reluctant guitarist
picks 70's tunes in the background.

Soon a group of cheerful women join a single man.
All drink cold beers and lip-sync with the songs in the air.
The waitress tucks her stringy hair behind her ears,
sighs, and takes their orders.

We listen for a while to the music –
enjoying our weekend escape and each other.
Now we sit in white wicker chairs
beneath the live oaks while a cool breeze
blows on this hot summer night in Calvert, Texas.

In the Heat of the Day

Instead of sitting on my couch this afternoon,
I decided to walk in the heat of an August day
in Texas -- feels like 106°, the temperature reads.
I dodged the tree shadows
to feel the sun on my bare arms and legs.
I'd rather hear the chirping cicadas,
the singing birds,
the laughing children
playing in the neighborhood park
than a blaring TV show on Netflix.
Three brown men speaking Spanish
on a roof are hammering shingles in place.
Two sons are sweeping out their parents' garage.
An old couple are making decisions
about paint for the gutters.
No one else seems to be moving
along in outside-freedom
except two little girls on pink bicycles
wearing Finding Dory backpacks
around their skinny shoulders.
They talk casually as I pass
of faces and whip cream pies.
I round the corner and walk
through my back yard
where I pick ripe grapes
from the vines growing
on the back porch arbor.

On the San Antonio Riverwalk

I cannot hold a table for four,
just me with no food,
so I am joined by three others
and the pigeons.
Two ducks swim in the murky water –
leaves and trash from abandoned lunches,
dropped by the breeze onto the surface.
A tour boat full of passengers parks inches away;
they disembark awkwardly close.
Now two young girls have taken the place of the three and
eat Asian noodles in silence,
avoiding my presence beside them.
In the air music mixes with the bird's chirping, boat motors,
and laughter.
Without warning, a trumpeter
removes her instrument from its case and
plays a tune for her friends and anyone else
who stops long enough to listen.
I find peace, sitting here alone and ignored,
watching strangers move to the rhythm of their lives.

Abandonment

When you walked to the car
this afternoon with your eyeliner
swirled dark and sharp in the style
so common these days among young girls
with piercings and a desire to be unique,
I spoke too quickly – as I always seem to do –
about *shouldn't you's* and *maybe you should's*
only to see you melt in the front seat,
your eyes now criticizing the image
you tried so carefully to create.

You greeted me just this morning,
copper hair flowing brightly across your shoulders,
eyes – perhaps I imagined – pleading
for affirmation and security,
knowing I am a safe place –
perhaps – too safe.

I'm trying to fill a role I have been forced to abandon,
yet I continue to play the part,
only occasionally switching characters
to appease you
or give myself peace –
false, at best.

Ten Steps Ahead

You walk ten steps ahead
of your texting son
because you don't think about
"he's not going to be 14 forever."
You think about the dentist visit
that took away an hour of your work.
You think about the nap you want
to take in your recliner
when you get home.
You walk proudly
in your fitted white shirt
and think about the workout
you had this morning at the gym
while your son was eating breakfast at home.
Sometimes we think today lasts forever.
We forget that soon tomorrow will be today
and today will be yesterday.

Rights

Stay right on 70E,
right on 44,
right on Jefferson.
You'll end up right on Park Avenue,
right before dusk,
right before dinner.
You'll call *Vin de Set* right before
too late to make reservations.
If you leave right now,
you'll be seated on the rooftop,
right where you want and
order just the right entrée,
eating right past satisfied.
You'll walk right back to your
B & B where the cool night is
just right for sitting in the garden and
talking about what's right with
your world, your 30-year (today) marriage.
Then you'll walk right upstairs and
end the night in just the right way.

From the Balcony

A goldadoodle owns the B & B
where we spent last night.
This morning he shook his wet fur
after drinking from the fountain
in the garden, cooling himself
from the game of catch
he played with one of the guests.

Across the street other dogs,
not so lucky,
walk their people,
pulling them impatiently by leashes
they hold in their hands,

and I watch from my seat
on the balcony outside our bedroom,
listening to the birds sing in the trees and
Nora Jones croon through the speakers.

FIERCE LOVE

Each morning, I stand at your closed door
with hands and heart lifted.
I will not let you go.
I have loved you long and fiercely –
a protector, a mother.

The time has come for you to leave;
I will release you.
I will not stop you, I cannot, from walking
into danger, from living only in
the moment, from ignoring the
Light that surrounds you.

With love and in faith I open my arms
and watch you walk away.
With hope I wait
for redemption and restoration.
In prayer I ask for
grace and mercy and peace.

MISCELLANEOUS

Being Mindful or How to Enjoy Your Day

Leave early and walk to class,
slow your pace just a bit,
feel the confident earth
firm beneath your feet.
Inhale, two, three, four.
Exhale, two, three, four.
Listen to the birds singing,
listen to the chimes ringing,
hum a tune,
or whistle.
Join the laughter of classmates,
watch silly squirrels
chase each other's tails,
the dog stop on his walk
to mark the moment.
Inhale, two, three, four.
Exhale, two, three, four.
Smell the warmth of coffee
you hold in your hands,
the sweet, smoky barbecue
foreshadowing lunch.
Inhale, two, three, four.
Exhale, two, three, four.
Eat an apple,
feel the juicy crunch
between your teeth,
lift your face to the sun,
feel the luxurious warmth
on your skin.
Inhale, two, three, four.
Exhale.

The Pig House

Blue pigs, pink pigs, yellow pigs;
purple pigs, white pigs, clay pigs;
metal pigs, spotted pigs, flying pigs.
Pigs in flowerbeds,
pigs under oak trees,
pigs on the porch,
pigs beside the back door,
pigs in flower hats,
pigs in bowties,
pigs carrying baskets,
pigs in sandals and shades.
Oink-oink, think the pigs.
Woof-woof, bark the dogs.
Hush-hush, yell the people.
Thump-thump, sound my shoes
as I run past the pig house
this quiet afternoon.

Siri

Sometimes Siri is my Muse.
Sometimes she is the fingertips God.
She changes *nemesis* to *memories*.
She changes *restore* to *re-store*.
She adds a hopeful emoji when I press a red-faced, horn-headed devil.
She says, "I'm sorry. I don't understand" in the middle of my rant.
BTW, she changes *rant* to *rent* —
a blatant reminder that anger does not pay what's owed.

Garage Sales

On display is the closeted proof
of a life lived not simply enough:
magazines unread,
clothes with price tags still hanging,
t-shirts of the glory days,
cosmetics tried and discarded,
jewelry never worn,
mugs, so many mugs.
But the people come
to gather the rejected tangibles
of someone else's excess.

Private Doors and Chalk-Drawn Squares

We live in boxes
behind private doors and
legal silences for the sake
of propriety, freedom, independence, individuality.
Nevermind the cries of anguished drowning.

We play games within the chalk-drawn squares.
Ignore the pleading eyes, hands outstretched –
no touching lest we lose our footing,
no leaning lest we fall onto each other.

Oh, for the rain to wash away the lines.

SAVED IN AMERICA

During World War II people were transported
by cattle cars to what some might call
God-forsaken hellholes, loaded like animals,
their luggage thrown into piles and burned.

In the 21st-century, July 2017, to be exact,
over one hundred adults and children were loaded
into a stifling tractor-trailer
and surely promised freedom and plenty in the land
of the free and the home of the brave --

young people like the ones I teach
and women like the one who
stops at my garage sale
to buy clothes for family in Mexico
because there are no jobs.
Grown men like the ones who cut my neighbors' grass
and young men like my son who just finished
his freshman year in college.

Thirty-eight were discovered. This morning.
In a Walmart parking lot.
Traumatized, disoriented, and dehydrated.

When the police opened the doors,
bodies, minds, and spirits
were found damaged by deprivation.
Eight were already dead.

And here I sit in my neighborhood Walmart parking lot,
in a cool car, sipping a Cold Brew from Starbucks
and mourn the horror. In my state.
My God, three hours from my front door.

MAYBE . . .

. . . if I could leave the shavings where I tried to make my
pencil sharp-ready
or the sticky spot on the carpet without scrubbing with white
foam
or leave the black, greasy smudges on the shower floor
or let the clothes rest unfolded in the basket
or the dishes unclean in the sink,
I could craft a poem worthy of your eyes.

. . . if I could leave the bed clothes unmade, rumpled,
they could mingle with ours
and I would feel the cool of your skin
and the warmth of your breath in the early afternoon
while the sun still streams through the open curtains
of our bedroom window.

ART

Art
is
often
created
in
the
middle
of
destruction –
maybe
art
is
humanity's
reminder
that
the
soul
cannot
be
destroyed,
that
the
expression
of
the
self
is
a
preservation
of
life.

BLOWING BUBBLES

Every city has one,
or should:
a man leaning
over a bridge
blowing bubbles
onto boat
passengers below.
Nothing but blue sky and
translucent bubbles that shine
with color in the sun's reflection.

Part II
Traveling

Flight

Seat 24B

In Group 3, Seat 24B
turbulent air shifts me
between the zones
of reality and dreaming,
not the way I imagined
our 30th anniversary flight –
you in the seat behind me,
only your knee pressed
to my back,
cloth and metal frame
between us,
a distance greater than
the motion discomfort bag
in the seat before me.

Waste Receptacles

The last time I used a lavatory
was somewhere over the Atlantic,
maybe between Dubai and Dallas.
Forgetting my shoes under the seat
in front of me, I walk there now,
the smooth floor – dry and clean –
under my feet, unlike the
long drops in Kenya or the squatties
I will soon see in China.
Returning, I give brief pause to quell my stomach
from the turbulence and reach
for the motion discomfort receptor
in my seat pocket
while the woman on my left
reads her Nook and
the man to my right flicks
a folded paper with his thumb and
looks impatiently around the cabin.

Sweeping in Dubai

In the Dubai airport this afternoon,
another student you might have been.
Instead, your broom circles around
the yellow cleaning sign placed
suspiciously near our group's rehearsal.
Glancing over your shoulder,
your arms in rhythm with our melody,
you pause often in your task.
What do you think as you search
for connection to the spirit in our song?
What are your dreams as you watch
the faces of those who are living theirs?
No smile flashes across your face,
just an acknowledging nod and
perhaps a longing for something more.

Flight to Shanghai

The lights are softly dimmed
above the too-loud roar of the engine,
heads tip sideways or
hang like ripe melons,
blankets rest casually
on laps and shoulders,
a few trays lie open
ready for the foil-covered
rectangles of half-heated seafood
left uneaten by gaping mouths
already full of sleep and recycled air.
The natives are restless –
bodies stir in cubicle-sized spaces,
eyes glaze with the fog
of time zone shifts,
screens glow with artificial light –
window shades slide up gradually
as weary faces seek the dawn.

Flight to Kenya

I
Luggage stuffed in bins
like the top of a matatu.
Bright bags, large bags,
small, and light bags.
Pale hands, dark hands,
frail, and strong hands.
There is room for everything –
all have a place.
Together the passengers work,
and passionately.
Life is bland if not engaged
wholeheartedly,
with the color of bodies and voices.

II
Flecks of light spatter
the ceiling like stars
in the night sky.
The cabin dims, heads nod.
Far ahead a child whimpers
in restless boredom
while her mother sits,
swaddled from frigid
vent wind and fights
the weight of sleep.
A few faces reflect
the screen glow,
zombie eyes wide
in sleepless seats
where elbows and knees
infringe on personal space.

A few voices soar
with the laughter of youth,
and young feet float
along the aisles.

Blank Verse

When from the window to the earth below
houses twinkle like pegs in a lite-bright
toy – a childlike attempt at artistry –
through clouds wispy white in the dawning day,
I wonder what world past this plastic pane
exists to move and breathe and live a life
of purpose, intent, and significance.
When from danger in the place I now sit,
a belt protects me through turbulent air
and trays are returned to their upright spots,
I hand my trash to the steward passing
and watch the passengers clutching their bags.
Alone, apart, and merely observing,
I ponder my role in the universe.

In Flight

A small child squirms
in her mother's arms –
trapped like the rest of us
in an airplane soaring
half across the world.

Some sleep, some dream,
others try to forget
the lives we've left behind –
the tasks undone,
the decisions weighing,
future plans as yet undetermined.

We watch make-believe people
leading artificial lives
on a screen only inches
from our mortal faces.

Meanwhile,
the child escapes and
toddles down the aisle,
just out of the grasp
of her mother's desperately reaching arms.

Flight of Fancy

"Just a minute, one last sip,"
you say of the life you hold
in your second clear plastic cup.
You've sat for two hours,
giggling, between two other 50+,
dyed-blonde women,
on your return to reality.
The flight attendant grows impatient
as you try to drain the dregs.
Abruptly, the plane's turbulence
forces the liquid up, out,
and onto your tight, white pants.
Now a red wine stain
spreads across the surface
of your fleshy thigh,
jarring you back to the world
you've escaped for a few short days.
No scrubbing will take away
the harshly visible color.
Soon you disembark,
watching your new friends rush,
smiling, to the arms
of their apparent families
as you walk– alone –
to reclaim your baggage.

CHINA

Suzhou Teacher Training: 3 Haiku

Desks form a horseshoe
name tags, pens, and empty chairs
a lonely room waits.

Ready for learning
supplies and lessons prepared
only five enter.

Breeze blows the papers
on the wall as rain splatters
against cloudy panes.

Rain Falls from Sky Like Blessings

We walk onto the slippery pier
like ripe vegetables wrapped in cellophane.
Drops scatter on the lake surface –
diamonds on glass.
Foggy air casts a dreamlike spell
as we walk on streets cobbled
with memories – wisdom of the past
soaks through our soles
like flowing river water.
We walk past ancient Gingko trees
whose roots bear pain of war,
past a washing stone worn smooth
by centuries of labor,
past open doorway through
winding alleys.
Private courtyards give glimpses
of life at Taihu Lake.
Till moon rises high,
we eat and sing round tables
spread with the feast of friendship.

Subway to Yushan Lu

Hands grip poles
to steady the jerky motions
of the ride to Yushan Lu.
A father holds close
the sleeping child,
adjusts the blanket
for imagined comfort.
Strangers turn the pages
of books or scroll screens,
eyes downcast to avoid distractions.
Curious residents watch
the foreigners swipe
through the doors
in a spirit of confident adventure.
A young man peels grapes
the size of ping pong balls
beside the subway door.
He shares with his mother;
they whisper softly and smile.

Eating Dumplings in Shanghai Airport

Mushroom pork dumplings
in the bamboo steamer
are no match for the ones served
at the village restaurant
near our hotel in Suzhou.
The people swarming by like locusts are not
the familiar faces of those who remain
to teach music and English
to the children of Lion Mountain,
the ones who will ride the subway
in the early afternoon to explore
a city of canals and ancient gardens,
shop for pearls and silk and souvenirs,
travel together to share a meal
of friendship and laughter with now-skilled chopsticks
before walking home again in the sticky air.

First Morning in Suzhou

The day breaks beneath a sky
overcast with clouds or smog,
vehicles honk impatiently on streets
already congested, the view from
our window cold and stark.
Concrete structures rise to breathe,
higher and higher.
Below, the people hurry to depart,
to arrive, to reach a destination
set for them, choice not a choice.
Eyes seek, hearts long
for the mystery just beyond their grasp.

The Color of Suzhou on a Sunday

So little color – drab blue or
the dull, steel gray of
concrete and metal,
an occasional splash of yellow,
equipment to build new structures
to fill with workers and empty people.
Even the sky is colorless,
a diffusion of smog that blocks the sun,
no birds – nowhere for them to fly,
to light. Clothes hang
over high rise balcony rails
to dry or fall on the streets
and alleys below.

El Salvador

Tito Drives Trucks

I sit beside a Salvadoran poem,
gray braid down the back of a red, plaid shirt.
With deep sighs, he rubs his eyes and glances
from window to brown hands that fidget between
a black bag and the tray table.
Tito drives trucks in Minnesota.
We chat easily as he speaks
sadly of "sights to break the heart,"
reality outside San Salvador Cathedral:
children sniffing glue for a cheap high,
prostitutes on the hunt for a quick dollar.
The difference is like night and day
from my country to his,
he says – incomparable.
By twelve the army pulled him to one life,
guerrillas to another –
wandering somewhere between,
he learned to distrust – but
tomorrow he will surprise his mother
with a mariachi birthday and
will gift his granddaughters
with the fruit of his sacrifice.

Aguilleres on a Sunday Morning

Voices rise in the sanctuary of
Iglesia Biblica Bautista
on this humid Sunday morning
in Aguilleres.
Laughter and rhythm pour from
musical hearts during these days
spent together in a country of
deep faith and generous hospitality.
Horse and rider pass by
church doors open to the dusty streets
where a woman scoops
diced vegetables into a plastic bag
with her hands and watches strangers
load into busses unfamiliar
in this peaceful Salvadoran village.

Basketball in La Palma

Six boys on a basketball court
freestyle a pick-up game of basketball.
Their youthful bodies run and
jump smoothly, freely in the La Palma air.
Unconcerned with the barrier of language,
a boy is drawn from a group
of passing tourists to join the players
for love of the game.
Hours pass, the sky darkens.
Shoppers disperse to their homes.
Still they play,
erasing the thin line between cultures.

Beautiful Cakes We Bought at the Market

Uneven, cobbled stones press into
the arches of our feet on our
walk to the supermarket in La Palma.
Water bottles keep sporadic rhythm in our backbacks.
From the meandering crowd
emerge Pedro and Miguel,
young boys who appear
in the most unexpected places:
a hike in the woods,
a drive to the Honduran border,
a celebration in the park,
a cardgame on the patio,
and now, here,
to carry the beautiful cakes.
Proudly, they hold up the rare treats and
say to each passerby –
"See what we bought at the market!"

On the Streets of San Salvador

Homeless people,
sprawl on the sidewalks
of San Salvador.
Tattered clothes,
laceless shoes, if any.
Some sleep
unaware of the colorful shirts passing
hurriedly, purposefully,
unscathed by empty stomachs.
Worn women,
press against graffitied walls;
hollow eyes wait for a coin, or two,
with open, hopeful hands and
search the sturdy shoes
that go by with full pockets,
healthy, strong legs
carrying them with focus
to the coolness of a flowered cathedral courtyard
on whose walls is hung the face of Christ –
inaccessible to the searching oppressed
just beyond the hope of this sacred space.

Santa Ana Winds

I
Cello, oboe, flute, voices –
in dissonant warmups –
notes rising in the open air church,
doors swung wide as trucks and
motorcycles pass unaware of the
strangers from far away
who gather to sing on
an early Sunday morning.
Hearty Salvadoran women prepare
pupusas across the tropical courtyard where
tables are spread with
hospitality –
the accordion dances a tango.

II
Young bodies leap in the pool
to catch a flying Frisbee
tossed in the Santa Ana sky –
a solitary pigeon sits
on the terra cotta roof and watches.

Malaysia

GOMANTONG CAVE

We washed our shitty shoes
over the squatty toilet –
buckets of water forced loose
the swiflets' droppings that stuck to our soles
as we walked through Gomantong Cave
where workers extract bird nests
for healing soup.
Mission belies the wealth of
brown bodies hanging over rails
before the entrance –
shirtless, cigarettes dangling,
a scarcity of activity at this time
before harvest in a rain forest in Sakau.

A Malaysian Countryside

A soft breeze stirs slightly,
challenging the oppressive humidity.
In the distance, a river runs in its muddiness
through the wild fronds of palm trees,
an eroding mountainside,
shoots of young palm trees
in this most rural Malaysian countryside –
a red clay path snakes,
the only break in the vast forest –
branches from a bush of yellow jasmine
hang heavy with fragrant blossoms.

Fresh Fish from the Sulu Sea

We needed 3 tables
to seat our group of 24
who sat white among the sea of Borneo residents.
Salty peanuts drop from our amateur chopsticks,
plates of crunchy noodles empty quickly,
we all compete for fresh papaya and pineapple.
In a dark back room an old woman sits on a stool
and bends over an aluminum tub to wash
the mountains of red plates that held so much food.
Silently, a skinny, tail-less cat creeps past.
In tanks behind us swim fins and claws
as our cameras flash to capture this night
rich with mystery of an unfamiliar culture.

View from a Mountaintop in Sapulut

The clouds hang low and
smoky this early morning
over a forest seen only this perfect
on a postcard in a tourist shop.
Below, the mighty river rushes
downstream with a steady *shhhhh*,
a reminder that peace is not without
movement or sound or surety of change;
sometimes peace is a wildness,
readying beneath a calm surface
to break forth in song of
insects, roosters, and youthful voices
eager to meet a new day.

Journey to Kudat I

Clouds darken the sky this afternoon
on the way to Kudat.
We pass cattle grazing freely
on the shoulder of the highway.
Banana trees and coconut trees
rise beside rice paddies
soaked in water from the frequent rains.
Political banners wave assertively in the breeze
over the roofs of dilapidated kiosks –
empty of produce grown locally
by farmers trying to feed their families.
Around the corner
a creek runs loudly
over rocks between two hills
covered with brilliant red hibiscus.
A rainbow arcs high
above a palm tree,
stiff green leaves droop
heavily in the humid air.

Journey to Kudat II

Wooden shanties covered with rusty
tin roofs line the trunk road
on the way to Kudat.
Shirtless men squatting beneath
coconut trees watch small, barefoot
children chasing tiny kittens.
Farther along, tired women wearing
the *tudung* provide for their families
by selling roasted corn, cassava chips,
and banana bunches, chopping blocks, fish traps,
and woven reed baskets.
As the sun sets, large vats of rice,
fish, tapioca root, and papaya
break the feast of Ramadan.

Kenya

Leaving Kenya

Reluctantly, we are done with
living out of backpacks and dufflebags.
Cramming onto vans with laughter
and singing and "baby goat" bleating.
Riding on bumpy roads, dust flying –
windows slamming shut, then open.
Watching the driver maneuver traffic
and near-death collisions.
Snacking on roasted peanuts, sliced sugarcane,
and honey purchased from vendors on the road side.
Painting the walls of AIC School for Girls,
surrounded by children wanting to help
wash the walls with rollers of color.
Speaking to a room stuffed full of girls
encouraged to hear that they can
"make a difference."
Sleeping on a makeshift pillow
and bare mattress in the abandoned mission house.
Walking up the Pokot hill on the rock-strewn path
to Mama Sheila's hut
where baby goats and children alike
make themselves at home.
Sitting on classroom benches in the Pokot schoolyard,
the sky brilliant with stars and hope.
Feasting on goat stew and *chapati*
cooked over an open fire by women
who have sacrificed time and sleep to welcome
friends from across the world.
Jumping with the Maasai in a mountaintop
church overlooking acacia trees and pasture land.
Dancing with African drummers and dancers
on a gravel driveway lit by carlight.

PERSPECTIVE

After a quick breakfast of bread and water,
the little boy runs to the field with his tree branch to herd
the skinny goats.

My son fills his stomach with "pancake on a stick" and
runs to the car to be on time for school.

A young girl escapes the hot afternoon under the shade of
an acacia tree
while her goats munch on the sandy stubble.

My daughter parks her car in the driveway,
pours a cold glass of apple juice, and
sits on the couch to watch TV.

The barefooted women fill their buckets with water from the
lake to use for
cooking and
      washing and
           drinking.

I turn on the kitchen faucet and let the water run.

Offering (with apologies to Christina Rossetti)

Four baskets held open –
    the people come.

What can I give, poor as I am?
Wearing colorful dresses their mommas made,
little girls giggle shyly to the front of the church;
old women in wrap skirts and head ties dance up the aisle exuberantly;
a father envelops his son's small hand and leads him --
some drop single coins in the hollow containers.

They lay before the altar
    a bottle of milk and
    a stalk of bananas,
    this family of five.
"Bananas are plentiful," they say.

If I were a shepherd, I would bring a lamb.
The village has slaughtered a goat for the welcome feast:
We gather around the fire of women squatting on stones to stir the stew and mix meal with precious water.
Kneading the dough with knobby hands, they place it proudly in the hot oil.
Soon plates are piled high with the cherished food.

If I were a wise man, I would do my part.
Eighteen suitcases stuffed expectantly
with t-shirts, underwear, soccer balls, and bubble gum.
We remove our baggage from the top of the bus in the dusty yard;

the treasures are extended with joy to the eager girls.

What I can I give?
Singing and laughing, we walk the dusty road to CuCu's house.
Her friends welcome us with brimming pots of *ugali*, goat, stews, and *sukuma wiki*.
Endless platters of bananas, watermelon, yams, and *chapati* pour from the kitchen all afternoon as we talk and eat.
We share and are satisfied.

I give my heart.

ugali – powdered maize boiled in water to become hard
sukuma wiki – cooked greens, similar to collards
chapati – fried bread

Ambush

We stuffed into our van this morning,
ready to experience nature on our first game drive of the day.

A brilliant sunrise,
The clack-clack-clack of male gazelle antlers asserting their young power,
A lone rhino spraying his territorial musk,
An elephant sucking up water in his long trunk and bringing it slowly to his thirsty mouth,
A herd of zebras striping the horizon.

Without warning, our driver killed the engine, and
we waited in silence.

Ten lions were strategically surrounding a young zebra,
separated from the herd.

Stealthily they drew closer,
ready for the kill.

Shrieks of pain died to moans as teeth tore the fresh flesh.
An adolescent lion tossed his head maniacally from side to side
as he tugged on the helpless hide, his wispy mane washed in the blood of the slain.

And we, since we were not the one dying, looked on –
intoxicated by death.

EVERY DAY I DREAM OF AFRICA

Every day I think of Africa and smell
    spicy pilau served at the Tocco's,
    the musky scent of a Kenyan friend,
    the earthy air of dust and animals as
        we drive through the countryside,
    the heaps of trash, animals, children, and
        old women at Nakuru dump.

Every day I think of Africa and hear
    children's laughter at Buckner Children's Home,
    joyous singing and ululations of Kenyan women,
    happy chatter of friends on our team van,
    desperate street people selling handmade
        crafts, fabrics, and souvenirs.

Every day I think of Africa and taste
    corn roasted over hot coals sold by street vendors,
    bland, sticky ugali served in large, metal pots,
    thick, rich goat stew cooked over an open fire,
    sweet, freshly cut mangos arranged
        temptingly on our breakfast platter.

Every day I think of Africa and see
    skinny children herding skinny goats in
        the barren fields,
    tired workers in the back of a truck
        after a hard day's work,
    village markets bursting with fruit,
        flowers, and furniture,
    sacrificial hospitality in the eyes of
        strangers who will quickly become friends.

Every day I think of Africa and feel
    raindrops splattering our faces on the safari van,
    cool, misty sunrises on the Tocco's back hill with
        coffee in one hand and a pen in the other,
    dust coating my skin as we ride the
        dry, rocky roads to Komolion school,
    the ache in my heart when I hug the
        handicapped orphans at Maji Mazuri.

Wishes Are Not Wings

You wash your child's hair
in a blue, plastic tub
under the acacia tree
on a cloudy afternoon,
and I wish for you
a sink so your back
will not stoop so low;
but you would not hear
the birds singing or see
the sun setting in
your African sky.
You spread your clothes to dry
on the *oleleshwa* tree,
and I wish for you a machine
to ease your task;
but you would not smell
the sweet scent of leaves
beneath your garments.
Your children kick the make-shift
soccer ball – plastic bags shaped
round and woven with ropes
by the hands of small boys –
and I wish for them a factory-made
toy to inspire their play;
but they would miss the skill
and pride gained from
creativity and resourcefulness.
I am drawn to your strength:
the acceptance of your situations,
the determination to overcome,
the confidence in your abilities together,
the joy in the blessing of living,
the trust that you are not alone.

So Funny, the Baboon

So funny, the baboon,
his fur-less bottom and skinny fingers!
Let's throw a pepper sandwich
on our way to Nakuru.
Watch the baboon take a bite,
spitting it out and flinging it away.
So funny, the baboon!
The memory of an elephant?
Ah, that of the baboon!
On our return to Nairobi,
let's toss another sandwich,
harmless, in good will.
Too late. The baboon remembers.
Jump attack, through the open window,
strangle-hold the sandwich-giver.
The end.
Not so funny, the baboon!

Circle of Life on Maasai Mara

Fifteen buzzards sit on a hill of the Maasai Mara
like bald-headed, skinny old men
passing time and waiting for action
at the town centre –
observant, expectant, but unhurried.
These scavengers watch as
three of their own hungrily pluck
the remaining flesh from a giraffe carcass
left in the ravine by a lion.
While we watch the scene unfold,
the breeze through the van windows
moves just enough to carry to our noses
the smell of this last supper
and to our ears the crunch
of brittle bones broken by hyenas
also enjoying the feast.
This is not an act of greed
but a violence expected, necessary
to balance nature and restore
the savannah to beauty and peace.

Rain over Ndondori Hills

Swollen rain clouds
roll in over Ndondori Hills
as thunder sounds
past the sunlight casting
shadows on the plain
painted with acacia and
cattle grazing gently.
Silver-back swallows dip their wings,
touch lightly on branches, and
rise again while frogs croak
on the path below my feet.
The solid rock warms beneath me;
I listen to the songs of nature.
In the distance, a drum beats,
a goat bleats, a child cries.

Buying Honey in Marigat

The old man sits on his *olorika*
under an acacia tree
watching visitors stopped by the roadside
to purchase honey
on their way to Nakuru.
Brown faces press against the pane.
Hands reach in
holding filled liquor bottles,
some small plastic.
Bees and honeycomb
swim in the golden liquid.
Money, smiles, and *asante sanas*
exchanged, the bus drives away
in the sunshine of morning.

Centre of Hope – Kibera, Kenya

Jambo, jambo bwana,
the children sang as we entered
the dimly-lit room and sat
on short blue plastic chairs.
Their eyes shone and voices rang
as their teacher beat the djembe,
baseball cap pulled low in
the style of a hip hop wannabe.
Soon we were led by guards
through the alleys of Kibera –
a parade of *muzungus* observing
the plight of the poor:
a boy sitting on a trash heap,
heels of his shoes digging
into crushed coal;
an old woman frying fish bones
in a pot of bubbling oil;
mounds of tomatoes and *sukuma wiki*
displayed for sale on wooden racks;
soggy papers mixed with mud and sewage;
a pan of potatoes, hot and crisp;
huddles of young men
looking for purpose.

Kibera Samosas

Stooped over a pan of bubbling oil,
an old woman patiently spreads
butter on thin sheets of dough
with her index finger.
Then, scooping up a mound of mashed peas,
she fills the thin pastry
and pinch-folds the edges –
bubble, bubble, sizzle, sizzle –
streams of grease drip from pot to plate,
samosas piled high and steaming.

Journey to Maasai Mara

Once again we cross
the swollen water
grown high from June rains.
Our van slides
on muddy road
while passenger heads
bounce up and down,
sided to side
like bobble heads
belted into seats.
Zebras lift their striped necks
and baboons, their fur-less
bottoms shining,
stop to watch our passing.

Journey to Komolion

Morop Hotel
Five doors conceal
empty rooms where
once a pallet refreshed
a weary traveler.
Blue paint peeling:
Baraka Trading, Cold Soda.
Chipped cement porch and
layers of dust beneath
a rotting, wooden table.

Termite Hills
Rising among
the scrubby bushes
powerful survivors,
timeless mounds
erect appendages
from Mother Earth.

Tortoise
Step by step,
slowly I turn,
hard shell hiding
a soft heart.
Sixty-nine hats
approach from behind –
the Paparozzi –
cameras flash,
excited voices whisper.
I withdraw my neck
and wait.

Balloon Safari

All night hippos
grunted and splashed
in Talek River.
Trusting and silent,
we gather to follow
a towering guard,
bright torch in hand,
down a still dark path
to the sound
of *whoosh, whoosh*:
an intermittent expulsion
of gas and fire
expands a massive
rainbow-colored fabric
spread across the ground.
In our basket we rise,
smooth and free,
to soar above
the grassy plain crisscrossed
with narrow animal trails.
The chill of morning melts
at the appearance
of a brilliant sunrise.
Elephants, giraffe, and
cape buffalo roam below,
unaware of human presence
except for the dark shadow
of our hot air balloon.

AMBOSELI
(for Daniel Sindiyo)

Fifty years ago
the acacia forest filled the plain
now bared by elephant hunger.
Our house once sat beside the pool
where lodgers, past and present,
cooled in the heat of day.
As now, frogs croaked in dark of night
and monkeys swung from trees,
hoping to grab a morsel from unsuspecting visitors,
who knew little of lions, giraffe, and rhino
that shared our spaces harmoniously.
Even a hyena could become a pet and
make memories with a boy grown now to be a man.
How fast fly the years –
when children wandered young and free.
Were our hearts lighter, life simpler?
Or has time merely softened
the sharp edges, the bumps and twists?
Can we now gaze across the horizon and
make memories with new friends and adventures?

Baboon at Fig Tree

Some Kenyans take their training
in universities and technical institutes;
others prefer a more experience-based approach.
Case in point: the clever
engineer at Fig Tree Lodge.
As dusk settles on the savannah and
hippos caroused in the Mara River,
a stealthy visitor approached an empty
room, moved the sisel mat,
unzipped the door, and entered.
Two backpacks, stuffed full,
lay seductively at the foot of the bed.
Oh, the scent of ripe apples –
irresistible!
Rip! Rip! Bite! Crunch!
Ah, the pleasure of forbidden fruit!
Toka!
      Kabisa!
The swat of a broom,
the kick of a boot on fur-less behind.
Oh, the price of forbidden fruit!

School Girl in Nairobi

What does the little school girl
think about in her light blue
jumper and yellow shirt –
threadbare navy sweater,
draped across bony shoulders?
Already too small, her thin shoes
wear a familiar path between school yard
and Athi River Concrete Plant.
Backpack – half zipped – carries
paper, pencils, and her favorite school book.
A skinny arm hooks elbows with a classmate
as they walk along and talk of what might be.
Quickly, she runs across the traffic and
descends a narrow path to her home of
cardboard lean-to's covered with pieces of tin.

Playing with Monkeys at Amboseli

Walking back to our lodge
on a sunny afternoon,
countless Vavert monkeys
dart playfully in the courtyard.
With slender fingers
they pluck clods of dirt
in search of insects,
stuffing in their mouths
blades of grass and bits of food
dropped by visitors
as they walk beneath the trees.
Sitting on a gnarled tree root,
one small fellow scratches
his belly with black-gloved paws.
Another chases his tail,
then holds it curiously.
The *click-click* of my camera
alerts some to potential danger or annoyance.
A black-masked monkey
with wisps of ear hair
rushes forward with outstretched arms.
Half-laughing, I jump backwards and
respect his territory,
which will remain long after I am gone.

African Rains

The school boy kicks his ball
high over the cattles' heads
in grass made green
by the African rains.

The teacher dips her bucket low
into the deep well
beneath water made high
by the African rains.

The woman dances in the courtyard,
head lifted to the sky
with face made joyful
by the African rains.

The farmer walks in his field,
gathering maize
made ripe for harvest
by the African rains.

The children run with bare feet,
toes squishing into the earth
made muddy
by the African rains.
All will rest,
stomachs satisfied
with food provided
by the African rains.

And all will rest
with the promise
of peace made possible
by the African rains.

Heat of the Day

In the heat of the day,
the animals seek shade in the tall grass
and we return to our lodge.
Some swim, others nap – I sit
beneath the shade of a jacaranda tree
and look out over the unfenced game reserve.
To my left a Maasai worker cuts the grass with a machete
and speaks Swahili into the cell phone pressed against his ear.
On the right a monkey munches on a lime, ignoring me.
Above my head African birds sing.
I listen to hippos grunt in the distance.

Elephant Challenge

Traveling a stretch of road in the Maasai Mara
where rhino are commonly sighted,
we encounter a family of elephants to the right of our safari van.
Alarmed at their closeness,
our driver commands complete silence.
Not even our young passenger is permitted to close his open window.
As we round the bend,
an adolescent male emerges from the tall bushes
and challenges us with his raised trunk,
moving a step towards us.
Determined, we inch ahead,
the elephant steps back –
one move forward, one step back,
forward, backward.
Finally, the road is cleared
and we can pass.
Not until we breathe again
do we consider the near-attack
from the defending adult elephants.

COLORADO

Settlers Loop

Before the Penny family
settled in the 1920s,
Colorado's indigenous
Ule Indians
enjoyed this rich land
of alpines, aspen,
and spruce
in the forests
along the mighty river
that supplies hydration
for both human and plants.

Now at the top
of Settlers Loop
sits a replica of an old log cabin
with grass sod roof
where deer come freely
in the heat of day
to rest on the cool dirt floor
of man-made dwellings
rather than in familiar,
untamed forests,
which exist less and less.
We have become
comfortable
to enter their habitats
which we strip and tame
for the sake of progress
and our own desires.
We've run them out of

house and home –
the native people and
the deer -- manipulating with blind hands
the mysterious loop of nature.

Bat of Darkness

Six flower boxes brighten
a black iron fence
surrounding the patio
this cool June afternoon
at Hawley Court.
Red geraniums,
yellow marigolds,
purple petunias,
and white miniature violets
lift their faces to the sun
in praise of freshness and light.
I, too, have been raising
my sights to the air above
in release and trust.
Stretching my legs,
my shoe brushes
across an object
on the stone,
creating a paper-thin rustle.
Small as a miniature toad
or giant horsefly
is a little bat – dead and dry –
lying in *shavasana*
on the cold stone,
arms outstretched
and tiny black wings
extended stiff and hard.
With protruding ears,
fleshy lips, and
matted olive-brown fur,
he seems ready
to fly again.

But he is lifeless –
prostrate and breathless.
Darkness and death,
light and life
coexist on this
ordinary summer day.

Mountain High

Rays of sun through the slats
in the wooden blinds
wake me at sunup.
Soon I am outside
walking briskly around
Settlers Loop.
I climb a hill less traveled,
breathless – from the altitude,
my pace, or the view.
What I see is not what I've seen:
Aspen and Spruce so tall
I nearly fall backwards
when I lift my head to the top.
The only sounds the birds and cicadas,
breeze passing through the branches,
and my own heavy breathing.
Whittaker Walk takes me
down some stone stairs
to the cool shade of a trail.
I walk past beds of flowers–
purple, pink, yellow, and white.
A wooden fence lines the trail
beside houses and into the thickness
of a flower forest
where a frog croaks
in alarm and butterflies
swarm around my head.
At a break in the trees,
a distant mountain range appears
capped with snow.

I stop for a long moment.
Dandelions and bumblebees scatter
as I finally turn to return
to the place I began.

Morning at Hawley Court

The sun rose this morning
to the wonder of daybreak,
peeping leisurely
over the chalk-trunk aspen
to breathe the fresh,
cool mountain air,
where deer sip dew
from blades of grass
beneath the open window
and birds wake
each other with unrestrained song.
Nothing is for show,
only a worshipful response
to the wonder of life,
to the beauty of creation
that proclaims the generosity
of a loving creator.

THE SOUTH

Wooded Secret

Pushed back from the road
like a secret,
an old, abandoned house
hidden among pine trees
catches my curiosity,
and I step off the path
tempted by the mysterious.
Moist, dark wood
choked by kudzu and harsh vines
winds around the chimney
and through the windows.
The tin roof still intact
like a responsible parent caring for the family.
The dilapidated porch caving in
surely houses snakes and vermin--
a voiceless shell of a home,
a time capsule
of untold stories.

Off Highway 106

So green the pine trees,
rising high to the sky,
Kudzu wrapped around fences,
trees, and electric light poles,
grasses and brown pine needles
on the roadside bedding
Easter lilies, mimosa blossoms,
crepe myrtle, and wild daisies.
Barbed-wire fences
holding back lazy cattle
grazing in the pasture,
a babbling brook
beside a pond laden with lily pads.
Old abandoned house, rusty mailbox,
empty rockers on the porch
inviting passersby to sit awhile and listen.
Bales of hay rolled in an open pasture.
Birds flying high. Hawks, crows, and songbirds
dipping their wings and singing praises
to the bright summer morning
and to each other.
A rain shower falling through moist air
like a tropical rain forest in Alabama.

Butler County 59

Aw! The memories on this road!
Early morning walks with the sun shining
on pine tree branches so thick
with kudzu you never feel
the rays on your skin.
Swallowed by a forest of oak, magnolia, and mimosa,
you round the corner where the rent house sits and
realize there is life after all in these woods
where cicadas chirp, birds sing, frogs croak,
cows gather for breakfast
in an overgrown pasture
that hides all but their moos,
and butterflies light on your arm
just long enough to feel a soft tickle.
At the bottom of a hill,
a creek flows fast and loud
against the backdrop of a lily-padded pond.
A soft breeze stirs the clouds high above.

Summer Haiku

Hidden among pines
A dilapidated house
Abandoned, alone.

Cows gather to feed
On my morning walk with Jack,
Brave dog he is not.

Summer dawn in June
Dew drops sparkle like gemstones
Birds sing harmony.

Sounds of the South

The *"Bob WHITE"* of
quails in the early morning.
Crickets chirping in the trees.
Frogs burping, swishing pond water
as they swim.
Crows cawing in the hayfield.
Squirrels climbing tree branches and
brushing their tails against the bark.
Horseflies buzzing around sweaty heads.
The whisper of mimosa trees
swaying in the hot breeze.
Pinecones popping and crunching
beneath pounding feet on hot pavement.
A four-wheeler rushing past.
White, shirtless boys
waving arms in the air,
hair plastered back with the wind.

Jogging with Jack

Feels like an Irish morning
in Alabama,
cool and quiet on this narrow lane,
a mysterious vacant house,
cicadas singing,
doves mourning,
a rich heady smell that goes deep,
green pastures,
a good dog,
a slow and simple pace –
peace, contentment, now.

Picking Kumquats on New Year's Eve

When I walk across the yard to the kumquat bush,
wet leaves stick to the bottom of shoes
I borrowed from Nanny's back porch.
The sky is a palette of gray,
no sun, no clouds.
Guns echo in the air –
rap, rap, rap, rap, rap.
The deer run desperately through the woods
to escape the hunters.
I pluck a kumquat –
rap, rap!
Orange globes of tartness –
rap, rap!
Life splashes on my tongue –
vibrant, sweet.
I spit the fruit flesh on the ground
where it will soon rot
like the animal carcass now lying in the back field.

CPSIA information can be obtained
at www.ICGtesting.com
Printed in the USA
LVHW091338011119
636075LV00009B/122/P